THE HIP-HOP REVOLUTION

CARDI B

BREAKING BOUNDARIES AND RECORDS

TERRI KAYE
DUNCAN

Enslow Publishing
101 W. 23rd Street
Suite 240
New York, NY 10011
USA

enslow.com

Published in 2020 by Enslow Publishing, LLC.
101 W. 23rd Street, Suite 240, New York, NY 10011

Library of Congress Cataloging-in-Publication Data

Names: Duncan, Terri Kaye, author.
Title: Cardi B : breaking boundaries and records / Terri Kaye Duncan.
Description: New York : Enslow Publishing, 2020. | Series: The hip-hop revolution | Audience: 5 | Includes bibliographical references and index.
Identifiers: LCCN 2018044066| ISBN 9781978509634 (library bound) | ISBN 9781978510005 (pbk.) | ISBN 9781978510012 (6 pack)
Subjects: LCSH: Cardi B, 1992—Juvenile literature. | Rap musicians—United States—Biography—Juvenile literature.
Classification: LCC ML3930.C255 D86 2020 | DDC 782.421649092 [B] —dc23
LC record available at https://lccn.loc.gov/2018044066

Printed in the United States of America

To Our Readers: We have done our best to make sure all websites in this book were active and appropriate when we went to press. However, the author and the publisher have no control over and assume no liability for the material available on those websites or on any websites they may link to. Any comments or suggestions can be sent by email to customerservice@enslow.com.

Photo Credits: Cover, p. 1 Ethan Miller/Getty Images; p. 5 JStone/Shutterstock .com; p. 6 MTV/TRL/Getty Images; p. 8 lev radin/Shutterstock.com; p. 11 Astrid Stawiarz/Getty Images; p. 13 Frazer Harrison/Getty Images; p. 14 Jared Siskin/Getty Images; p. 17 Kevork Djansezian/Getty Images; p. 18 Kathy Hutchins/Shutterstock .com; p. 21 Axelle/Bauer-Griffin/FilmMagic/Getty Images; p. 23 Nicholas Hunt/Getty Images; p. 24 Roy Rochlin/FilmMagic/Getty Images; p. 26 Ilya S. Savenok/Getty Images; title graphics (arrows) Vecster/Shutterstock.com.

CONTENTS

LIFE IN THE BRONX

On October 11, 1992, a baby girl was born in the Bronx. The Bronx is the northernmost part of New York City. More than half of the area's population has a Latino or Hispanic background. And like so many in the area, this baby's parents have Latino roots, too. Her father is originally from the Dominican Republic. Her mother is from Trinidad. They named their child Belcalis Marlenis Almanzar. Little did they know at the time what a deep impact their little girl would grow up to have on the Bronx and hip-hop culture as Cardi B.

GROWING UP POOR

Belcalis did not have an easy life. Though her parents were hard working, they did not make a lot of money. Everyday life was difficult for the family, which

Cardi B attends the Tidal X: Brooklyn concert on
October 17, 2017, at the Barclays Center.

also included Belcalis's younger sister, Hennessy Carolina. The family first lived in the Washington Heights neighborhood. They moved to the Highbridge neighborhood in the South Bronx when Belcalis was

Hip-Hop History

It was in the Bronx in 1973 that rap music and hip-hop began. DJ Kool Herc, the father of hip-hop, had back-to-school parties. At these parties, he spun records on two turntables. He also spoke into the microphone while the music played to keep the party going.

Cardi B (*right*) and her younger sister, Hennessy Carolina, visit the MTV show *TRL* on April 10, 2018. Hennessy is an Instagram celebrity with millions of followers.

in sixth grade. She still spent a great deal of time with her grandmother, who remained in Washington Heights.

When Belcalis was just thirteen years old, her parents separated. Life was even more challenging for a single mother with two young daughters. Highbridge was a tough neighborhood with a high crime rate. There were drugs and gangs. Violence was common. It was not easy raising children in that environment. Belcalis's mother was quite strict as a result.

Belcalis and her sister were not allowed to attend parties at night. They were also not allowed to go to sleepovers because their mother could not be sure who might attend the overnight gatherings. Additionally, Belcalis suffered from severe asthma. Her mother worried constantly that an asthma attack would mean a hospital stay for her fragile little girl.

"Family is my peace of mind. I love my family."[1]

But Belcalis soon figured out a way to get around her mother's rules. Since she could not go out at night, she sometimes went to get-togethers held at a friend's apartment during school hours. Friends and fun were more important to her than school!

Cardi B performs at the Global Citizen Festival in New York on September 29, 2018. She's loved the color red since she was a teenager and wears it often.

A TALENTED TEEN

What Belcalis lacked in money, she made up for in personality. She had a sassy attitude, was funny, and was popular among her friends. She was also very proud of her Caribbean roots. In fact, she was raised bilingual; she can speak Spanish and English.

From a young age, Belcalis felt destined to be creative. She attended Renaissance High School for Musical Theater and Technology. Here, the smart, witty high school student had an opportunity to showcase her blossoming entertainment skills. She participated in talent shows and was cast in musicals. At one talent show when she was sixteen, Belcalis performed a Lady Gaga song. She wore a bright red jumpsuit and had an entire crew of backup dancers. Already, she had a presence on the stage. The audience cheered and applauded her performance. This was just a hint of what the future would bring.

Belcalis was also very social. In fact, she preferred spending time with her friends to studying or attending rehearsals for school musicals. Though she had the potential to be a very good student, she sometimes neglected her grades. Belcalis liked to be in the loop. She wanted to know what was going on with her friends and wanted to be a part of the social scene at her school. This did not mean that Belcalis did not value education, however. She knew that furthering her education was a way to escape the poverty that she had known all of her life.

A BETTER WAY

2

After she graduated from high school, Belcalis enrolled at Borough of Manhattan Community College. She studied French, Western civilization, and American politics. At the time, she thought she might one day become a history teacher.

While attending college, Belcalis also worked at a supermarket. She wanted to help her family financially. However, she soon discovered that working and attending college was very stressful. She dropped out in order to focus on other ways to earn money and make her way in the world.

SOCIAL MEDIA STARDOM

By the time she left college, it was mostly only family who referred to Belcalis by her given name. To the rest of the young woman from the Bronx was making a name for herself on social media as Cardi B. She was no longer attending college or working at the super-market. Instead, she was working hard to promote

"It's hard to think about fulfilling your dream when you got so much responsibility. Your responsibilities come first."[1]

herself on sites such as Instagram. Using social media, she expressed her opinions and thoughts through short, fifteen-second "tirades" and "tell it like is" videos that were also funny. Soon, Cardi B had a large online following.

Cardi B visits the SiriusXM Studios in New York City on April 10, 2018. Her honesty and humor made her famous. During interviews, she still speaks her mind.

A Name Destined for Fame

Cardi B's parents nicknamed her Bacardi to honor their backgrounds. Bacardi is a popular adult drink that was first made in Cuba, one of many islands in the Caribbean. Over the years, Bacardi was shortened to Cardi. She added a "B" to show how she felt about herself—bold, beautiful, and more!

Cardi B was not afraid to speak her mind. She was opinionated, and on her social media sites, she was very outspoken. Some of her posts went viral, which made her a celebrity. Not everyone was positive, however. Some people viewed her sites and were unkind and judgmental. This did not deter the hard-working, determined girl from the Bronx. She believed in herself and did not give up.

As Cardi B's social media fame skyrocketed, she decided to follow the recommendation of a longtime friend and supporter and focus more on creating rap music. She reflected on her life experiences and began rapping about the struggles she faced growing up without much money. Her music had a strong Caribbean

Cardi B performs at the Coachella Music and Arts Festival on April 22, 2018, in California. Her rap career began after she reached internet fame.

influence. Her strong Spanish accent was also reflected in the way that she pronounced some words in her songs. Cardi B stayed true to her Bronx roots with the music she created. People listened, and they liked what they heard.

MAKING A SPLASH ON THE RAP SCENE

Cardi B grew up listening to music. Some of her favorite artists included pop stars such as Madonna and Lady Gaga. She was also a big Beyoncé fan! The first albums

Cardi B poses with fellow female rapper Missy Elliott at a pre-Grammy party in 2018. Elliott was one of Cardi B's role models growing up.

she purchased were by Missy Elliott and another by Tweet, both successful female artists. Cardi B's rap style, however, was more influenced by musicians with a Caribbean sound such as Puerto Rican rapper Ivy Queen and Jamaican artist Spice.

Cardi B's rap music style attracted the attention of other musical artists. In November 2015, she made her musical debut by joining a well-known Jamaican reggae artist, Shaggy, on a song. In December of that same year, she became a regular cast member on the reality television show *Love & Hip Hop: New York*. That was just the beginning of Cardi B's rise to fame! At just twenty-three years old, Cardi B was already a shining star!

Though Cardi B was a woman competing in a musical field traditionally dominated by men, she was determined to succeed. She believed that women could accomplish just as much as men. Some people, though, did not believe that she could do that. Cardi B set out to prove those people wrong. It did not take long for her to do so.

RAPPING HER WAY TO THE TOP

Despite her early success, Cardi B sometimes suffered from low self-esteem. There were times when she felt that she was not good enough. She was also sensitive about the way she looked. In order to boost her self-confidence, she made the decision to invest in herself. She believed that improving her looks would help her become a more successful celebrity. Cardi B decided to undergo several cosmetic procedures, including extensive dental work to straighten her crooked teeth.

The rapper and social media star was very open and honest about her decision. Though some people made mean remarks about her choice, Cardi B tried to ignore the body shaming. She knew that she felt better about herself and felt prettier.

Cardi B walks the red carpet at the American Music Awards on October 9. 2018, in Los Angeles, California. She won for favorite rap/hip-hop artist.

MAKING IT TO THE BIG TIME

In March 2016, Cardi B released a full-length project of her best work on a mixtape. This allowed her to capture the attention of even more listeners. Soon, she was working with other major artists, appearing on the cover of a magazine, and working on her next mixtape release. It was a busy year for Cardi B, but it was just the beginning.

In August 2017, Cardi B performed her soon-to-be hit single "Bodak Yellow" at the MTV Video Music Awards.

Not long after Cardi B released her second mixtape in January of 2017, she announced that she had signed a major record deal with Atlantic Records, one of the most well-known record companies. Her debut studio single, "Bodak Yellow," was released on June 16, 2017. By late September, the song was number one on the US Billboard Hot 100 chart! Cardi B was only the second female rapper to accomplish this with her first single! Her song stayed at the top of the chart for three straight weeks. This tied the 2017 record previously held by pop sensation Taylor Swift. "Bodak Yellow" was described

"Remain humble but stay hungry."[1]

by some as "the rap anthem of the summer."[2] It eventually sold millions and millions of copies.

The year 2017 has been described by some as "the Year of Cardi B."[3] In addition to successfully releasing more of her own music and signing a record deal, she appeared on television shows such as *The Tonight Show*. She graced the cover of magazines such as *New York* and *Rolling Stone*.

Awards and award nominations were piling up, too. Cardi B even performed at the MTV Video Music Awards. She was proving to the doubters that success could indeed happen to those who truly put in the work.

Making History

Cardi B was the first person of Dominican descent to have a song hit number one in the history of the Billboard Hot 100 chart. The Hot 100 chart was originally launched in 1958. Where songs place on the chart is based on radio play, online streaming, and sales in the United States.

By the time Cardi B's debut album, *Invasion of Privacy*, was released in April 2018, the megastar had much in her life to celebrate. Two other songs from the debut album climbed to the top ten spots on the Hot 100 chart. This made her the first female artist to ever achieve such an accomplishment on the Hot R&B/Hip Hop Songs chart. She had been nominated for numerous awards, including two Grammy Awards, and had won multiple Black Entertainment Television (BET) Awards.

A FAMILY OF HER OWN

However, not all of the accomplishments in Cardi B's life related to her stardom. In April 2018, she announced that she was going to have a baby. She also revealed that she had secretly married her boyfriend, hip-hop

Cardi B and Offset were secretly married in September 2017. Offset, whose real name is Kiari Kendrell Cephus, is a rapper from Lawrenceville, Georgia.

artist Offset of the trio Migos, the previous September in Atlanta, Georgia, at a private ceremony! On July 10, 2018, she gave birth to a little girl they named Kulture Kiari Cephus. In late 2018, Cardi B announced that she and Offset broke up.

STAYING ON TOP

Without question, Cardi B is a true Bronx-style Cinderella story. The little girl raised in poverty is now a huge success. She is able to provide for her family. Though she loves her career, she does admit that it can be exhausting. On the rare days that she has off, Cardi B enjoys staying home and relaxing. She is a New York City girl at heart who has never gotten a driver's license and who loves fast food from McDonald's.

THE BAD SIDE TO FAME

While success has brought Cardi B fame and fortune, she admits that there are times when she feels she sacrificed a degree of happiness to achieve all of her accomplishments. As a regular girl from the Bronx, she could do and say anything she pleased. Now she has to be much more careful about what she says. Though she says that she is the same person that she has always been, Cardi B sometimes feels like people love her only for her money and what she has become.

With success also comes pressure and critics. She often feels overwhelmed. Her goal was to make people laugh. She wanted to entertain people and showcase her talents.

Cardi B is a fashion icon with a unique style. She often attends fashion shows, like this one during New York Fashion Week in September 2018.

Cardi B attends the *America's Next Top Model* premier on December 8, 2016. She cast a former winner of the show in one of her music videos.

"If I change myself, then I'm going to lose myself, and I won't be who makes me happy."

Family Support

Cardi B's large and loving family provides a strong support system for her. She says her family is full of "jokesters" and that they love to laugh.[1] She grew up alongside thirty-six cousins. Most of them lived in the same building in the Highbridge neighborhood where she grew up.

Cardi B did not, however, sign up to be bullied. Though she tries to ignore her critics, she can't help but care what others think of her. While she is happy that she can take care of her family, she has paid a price. But there is no turning back.

REMEMBERING HER ROOTS

Cardi B is also very proud of who she is and said, "If I change myself, then I'm going to lose myself, and I won't be who makes me happy."[2] Her mottos are, "Do not apologize for what you are" and "Just be yourself."[3]

Cardi B has come a long way from her rough beginnings as a poor girl from the Bronx. She continues to work hard for her success.

She also believes that all people deserve to be respected. Cardi B hopes to reach people and spread her message in an entertaining way. She wants to show others that she is not just another girl from the Bronx who thinks she can be a big star on the big stage.

While Cardi B is a hard worker herself, she admires other women, such as her mother, who also work tirelessly to support their children. In the future, she hopes to have more children and provide them with a nice home and financial security, things she did not have growing up in the Bronx.

WORKING FOR THE FUTURE

Cardi B wants to make more hit records and try acting as well as designing clothes. She has a passion for making money and being responsible with it. She says that one of the most important keys to financial success is careful budgeting.

The possibilities for a driven, successful woman like Cardi B are endless! The opinionated city girl known for her unique style, bedazzled nails, and love of bright colors has no plans to stop. "This is my work ethic: I do not want to raise my future kids where I was raised, and I know the only way to do it is working, working, working, working, working."[4] She made it big despite the fact that the odds were against her. Cardi B's success continues to be an inspiration to others. As she reminds others, "Every little step is a big step!"[5]

TIMELINE

1992 Belcalis Marlenis Amanzar, later known as Cardi B, is born in the Bronx on October 11.

2015 By October, Cardi B has around 500,000 followers on social media sites such as Instagram and decides to pursue a career in rapping.

2015 Cardi B makes her musical debut with Jamaican reggae singer Shaggy in November.

2015 Cardi B makes her first television appearance on VH1's *Love & Hip Hop: New York* on December 14.

2016 Cardi B releases her first full-length project, a mixtape.

2017 Cardi B signs a major record deal with Atlantic Records in February.

2017 Cardi B releases her debut single, "Bodak Yellow," on June 16.

2017 Cardi B marries hip-hop artist Offset on September 20.

2017 "Bodak Yellow" is the number one song on the US Billboard Hot 100 chart in September.

2018 Cardi B releases her first studio album, "Invasion of Privacy," on April 6.

2018 Cardi B and Offset's daughter, Kulture Kiari Cephus, is born on July 10.

CHAPTER NOTES

CHAPTER 1. LIFE IN THE BRONX

1. "All the Times Cardi B Gave Us the Best Life Advice," Stars Insider United Kingdom, May 14, 2018, https://uk.starsinsider.com/celebrity/220885/all-the-times-cardi-b-gave-us-the-best-life-advice?.

CHAPTER 2. A BETTER WAY

1. Sarah Friedmann, "What Is Cardi B's Album Release Date? 'Invasion Of Privacy' Can Be Yours Sooner Than You Think," Bustle, March 27, 2018, https://www.bustle.com/p/what-is-cardi-bs-album-release-date-invasion-of-privacy-can-be-yours-sooner-than-you-think-8612681.

CHAPTER 3. RAPPING HER WAY TO THE TOP

1. Cardi B (@sheiscardi), "Remain humble but stay hungry," Instagram video, December 21, 2017, https://www.instagram.com/p/Bc87iG5lqhM/?hl=en.

2. Joanna Nikas, "An Afternoon with Cardi B as She Makes Money Moves," *New York Times*, August 17, 2017, https://www.nytimes.com/2017/08/17/fashion/cardi-b-bodak-yellow.html.

3. Brittany Spanos, "The Year of Cardi B," *Rolling Stone*, October 30, 2017, https://www.rollingstone.com/music/music-features/the-year-of-cardi-b-200589/.

CHAPTER 4. STAYING ON TOP

1. Chris Martins, "2017 No. 1s: Cardi B on Her Rise to Hot 100 History," *Billboard,* December 21, 2017, https://www. billboard.com/articles/events/year-in-music-2017/8071047/ cardi-b-hot-100-history-interview-no-1s-2017.

2. Samantha Schnurr, "Cardi B Turns the Tables on Those Offset Cheating Allegations: 'People Don't Know What I Did,'" E! News, February 27, 2018, https://www.eonline. com/news/916716/cardi-b-turns-the-tables-on-those-offset-cheating-allegations-people-don-t-know-what-i-did.

3. Amanda Leone, "Face It, Cardi B Is a Force to Be Reckoned With," Odyssey, October 26, 2017, https://www. theodysseyonline.com/why-cardi-is-force-to-be-reckoned-with.

4. Bang, "Cardi B Working to Make a Better Future," MSN Entertainment, December 21, 2017, https://www.msn.com/ en-sg/entertainment/celebrity/cardi-b-working-to-make-a-better-future/ar-BBH7UBi.

5. djvlad, "Cardi B: Money Doesn't Always Make Me Happy, I Understand Suicidal Celebs," YouTube, March 22, 2017, https://www.youtube.com/watch?v=2Teq5Aob_nA.

GLOSSARY

asthma A disease that causes the airways of the lungs to become swollen or inflamed, which makes breathing difficult.

body shame To criticize someone for his or her body type.

budgeting Setting aside a certain amount of money for something.

cosmetic procedure A surgical or nonsurgical process that changes parts of the body, often to improve appearances.

debut The first or earliest work.

dominate To control or have a commanding influence.

mixtape A collection of favorite pieces of music that an artist puts out without the help of a recording studio.

sacrifice Something given up or lost.

tirade A speech that can be angry or critical.

viral Fast-spreading on the internet.

FURTHER READING

BOOKS

Hill, Laban Carrick. *When the Beat Was Born: DJ Kool Herc and the Creation of Hip Hop.* New York, NY: Roaring Brook Press, 2018.

Llanas, Sheila Griffin. *The Women of Hip-Hop.* Minneapolis, MN: ABDO Publishing, 2017.

Morgan, Joe L. *Cardi B.* Broomall, PA: Mason Crest, 2018.

WEBSITES

Billboard: R&B/Hip-hop Music
www.billboard.com/hip-hop-rap-r-and-b
Check out the latest hip-hop news.

Kidzworld: Pioneers of Hip Hop
www.kidzworld.com/article/5321-pioneers-of-hip-hop
Find out how hip-hop and rap got started.

INDEX